The Hostel That Taught Me Life

A Seven-Year-Old's True Story of Friendship, Fear, and Change

Sravanth Killamsetty

BlueRoseONE.com
Stories Matter
NewDelhi • London

BLUEROSE PUBLISHERS
India | U.K.

BlueRose ONE
Stories Matter
NewDelhi • London

For permissions requests or inquiries regarding this publication, please contact:

BLUEROSE PUBLISHERS
www.BlueRoseONE.com
info@bluerosepublishers.com
+91 8882 898 898
+4407342408967

ISBN: 978-93-7542-700-1

Cover design: Rohit
Typesetting: Namrata Saini

First Edition: January 2026

Part 1:

A Seven-Year-Old's True Story of Friendship, Fear, and Change.

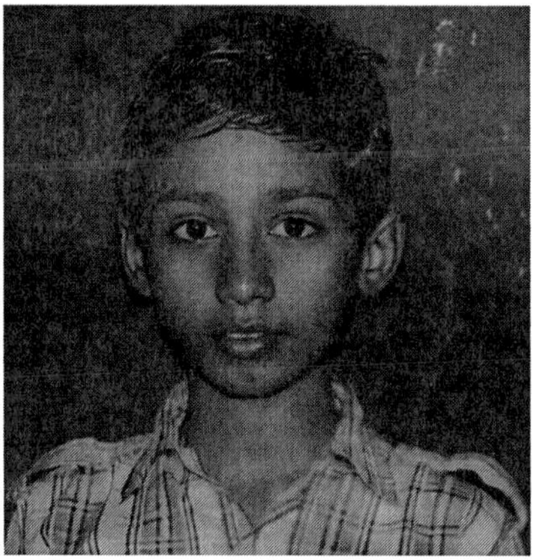

Dedication

To the friends who became family,

and to the boy I once was –

still laughing, still learning.

Acknowledgements

I owe my deepest gratitude to the people who shaped my journey and made "**The Hostel That Taught Me Life**"

First and foremost, to my parents, **Mr. Venugopal Rao Killamsetty and Mrs. Gita Killamsetty**, for their endless love, quiet sacrifices, and the values they instilled in me - long before I understood their depth.

To my brother-in-law, **Dr. Ravindra Nandhana**, and my sister, **Vijitha Nandhana**, for their constant support, encouragement, and belief throughout this journey.

To my younger self **Sravanth Killamsetty** (as Aarav in the story)

To my brother, **Praneeth Killamsetty** (as Vihan in the story)

To my childhood friends, who lived these memories with me and made hostel life unforgettable - Sampath, Akhil Sai, Akhil, Cherishma (as Zia in the story), Jayanthi (as Jayani in the story), and Sruthi (as Selena in the story)

and many more.

To my teachers, who not only guided my academics but also shaped my character -

1. Ms. K. Rekha (Principal)
2. Mr. Andhavarapu Anjaneyulu (Resident Director)
3. Ms. Sai Rani (Hostel Warden)
4. Ms. Bindu (Hindi teacher, 2008)
5. Ms. Sindhu (English teacher, 2008)

And many more to remember.

And every teacher who, in ways big and small, left an indelible mark on my journey.

To all of you -

this book is not just **mine**; it is **ours**.

Author's Note

And what more could a 3rd grade boy ask for than the journey he found within the walls of Sarvani Vidya Nikethan, Rajeev Nagar, Singupuram(PO), Srikakulam, Andhra Pradesh.

For me, those days were more than classes, books, and exams. They were laughter-filled nights in the hostel, whispers of secrets under dim lights, pranks that turned into lifelong memories, friendships that shaped who I am, and rivalries that pushed me to grow.

This was not just school - it was a stage, where every prank, every quarrel, every tear, and every cheer unfolded like a scene from a film.

And I was living it, not as an actor, but as a boy discovering life one moment at a time.

What else could a 3rd grade boy have? What else could a 7 years old boy could ask for?

A place where friendship is tested, where innocence meets ambition, where competition blends with care, and where every little experience becomes a story worth telling.

This is what a 3rd grade boy truly has.

This is what childhood should feel like.

And I believe, for anyone who has lived their school years deeply, this is the journey you too will recognize.

Because this isn't just my story - it's a real story. A lived story. A memory shaped in corridors, classrooms, and hostel dormitories. A story that, when told, must feel not less than a cinema - because every emotion was real, every bond unforgettable, and every farewell a truth of growing up.

This is **"The Hostel That Taught Me Life"**

Not just a book.

But an **experience**.

It's real incidents, real emotions, real scars, real laughter.

A note that this book isn't meant to glorify hostel life but to capture it raw - like cinema unfolding in words.

My story, It's all about **ME** in **YOU** somewhere.

Contents

Introduction

Some stories stay with us long after childhood ends. Some moments, some friendships, and some fears never truly leave. This is one such story.

At the age of seven, Aarav stepped into a world far away from home - a boarding school where courage was learned the hard way, laughter echoed inside cold walls, friendships were born in crowded dorms, and fears hid in every corner of the night. Between punishment and play, rivalry and love, mischief, and mistakes, he grew up faster than he should have, carrying emotions bigger than his little shoulders.

These pages hold the memories he lived between 2008 and 2010 - the three years that shaped him forever. Years that taught him what it meant to miss someone, to value family, to fight fear, to protect friends, and to understand bonds that feel like blood even when they are not.

Inside this book live the stories of late-night pranks, bathroom wars, movie evenings that ended too soon, friendships strong enough to fight loneliness, and silent promises made by a boy who only wanted to make his parents proud.

And yet, hidden beneath all the fun and chaos is a quiet truth: growing up in a hostel teaches you more about life than you realise. It teaches you to hold on. It teaches you to let go. It teaches you that time moves forward, but memories stay.

Today, as a grown man of 24, Aarav looks back at those three unforgettable years - sometimes with pain, sometimes with longing, always with love. He may have lost touch with many friendships, but the boy he once was still lives inside him, whispering stories he refuses to forget.

This book is that whisper.

A journey back to the rooms, corridors, fears, friendships, and magical moments that built the boy - and the man - he became.

Welcome to **"The Hostel that taught me life"**

A childhood remembered.

A heart rediscovered.

Chapter: 1
The Unseen Beginning

Every story has that one day when everything changes - the day you pack not just your bags but also your heart, and step into a world that doesn't smell like home anymore. For **Aarav**, that day had finally arrived.

He stood at the threshold of boarding school life, caught between the warmth of his family and the unknown chill of new beginnings. His heart was a mix of excitement and sorrow, as though he were both the hero of an adventure film and the child in a tearful farewell scene.

At times, he felt like the only boy in the world being exiled, carrying loneliness like a heavy schoolbag. But then he glanced at **Vihan**, his cousin and confidant - his fellow soldier in this battle of growing up. That bond was his anchor. After all, it's easier to face the storm when you know you're not the only one without an umbrella.

The gates of the boarding school opened wide, like the entrance to a new world Aarav never asked to enter. Tall buildings, long corridors, and a big playground filled with loud laughter and nervous whispers made everything feel like the beginning of a movie.

Aarav looked around, his heart caught between fear and curiosity. Beside him, Vihan stared just as wide-eyed. They exchanged a look that said everything - both scared, both unsure, but both knowing this was their new life now.

This wasn't a home with a **mother's soft voice or a father's warm presence**. This was a place of **bells, wardens, rules**, and **routines**.

Their parents stood close, smiling proudly even though their eyes showed sadness. They were letting go, hoping their sons would grow.

Aarav tried to be brave, telling himself that this was not being left behind but being given a chance. Vihan, on the other hand, held on to his parents as if he could stop time if he hugged hard enough.

In that moment, the difference between them was clear - Aarav was ready to try his wings, while Vihan was still holding on to the nest.

A Goodbye That Came Too Soon.

The rest of the day passed in a blur - new faces, hurried introductions, papers being signed, and clothes folded into small hostel cupboards that suddenly felt too big and too empty.

And then, the moment everyone had been pretending not to think about finally arrived.

Aarav tried to stand tall. He kept his face calm, his chin lifted, giving his parents small nods that silently said, "Don't worry. I'll be okay." But inside, his heart was shaking. He was only a boy, but he was already trying to act like a grown-up.

Vihan couldn't do the same. Tears streamed down his cheeks, each drop showing how much he didn't want this goodbye. His little body shook as he cried, and the sound of it felt like someone pressing a weight on Aarav's chest. Aarav wanted to cry with him - he always had. They were like two halves of the same heart. But this time, he forced himself to stay still. His eyes burned, but he blinked it all away. He had decided he would not break. Not here. Not in front of his parents. He wanted them to leave believing their son was strong.

Their parents hugged them one last time, whispered soft promises, and slowly walked toward the car. Then came a sound that would stay in their memories forever - the car door shutting, the engine starting, and the quiet roll of tires pulling away from them.

In that instant, something inside Vihan snapped. With all the strength in his small legs, he suddenly ran after the car. He didn't think - he just ran, as if the world would stop if he reached the car on time.

And without a second thought, Aarav ran after him. Two boys chasing after the last moments of childhood, chasing the people who made them feel safe.

For a few seconds, everything felt like slow motion. The wind against their faces, their feet slamming the ground, their hearts beating louder than anything else.

The driver noticed and stopped. The doors swung open again, and their parents stepped out with tears in their own eyes. They pulled the boys close - another hug, another kiss on the forehead, another chance to hold on before letting go.

But every goodbye must end.

Their parents got back in, the doors closed again, and this time, the car moved forward without stopping. Aarav and Vihan stood there in silence, their hands clenched, watching the car grow smaller and smaller until it finally disappeared.

And just like that, life moved them into a new chapter - one filled with **rules, bells, bunk beds**, and a **hundred emotions** they had never known before.

Stepping Into the Unknown.

As the car disappeared beyond the school gates, Aarav and Vihan slowly turned back toward the hostel. Their hearts felt heavy, their eyes still wet, but they had no choice - they had to move forward.

That evening, the playground became their escape. They ran around the slides, pumped their legs on the swings, and tried to laugh. Sometimes the laughter was real, sometimes it was just their way of hiding the pain.

Childhood has its own magic - even when the hurt is fresh, it finds little ways to heal.

Dinner in the mess felt strange. Plates clanged, students talked loudly, and the food tasted nothing like home. For Aarav and Vihan, it only made them miss home even more. Later, when they returned to their room, the two small beds stood side by side - close enough to feel safe, yet not close enough to replace the warmth of their parents.

When the lights went off and the dormitory turned quiet, both boys lay awake, staring at the ceiling. Their thoughts drifted home….to their mother's soft touch, their father's firm voice, the familiar comfort of a goodnight wish. Now, those memories felt far away - like stars in the sky… visible, but out of reach.

That night, silent tears soaked their pillows. They didn't speak. They didn't need to. Somewhere in the silence, one truth remained,

They still had each other.

And tomorrow… their **new life** would begin.

Chapter:2

The Beginning of Us.

The first day of school was not just about books. It was about starting something new, stepping into a place where strangers might soon become friends. Aarav felt like he was standing at the beginning of a film. He didn't know what was coming - maybe laughter, maybe fights, maybe moments he would never forget. Vihan felt the same.

That morning, both boys woke up earlier than usual. Their stomachs were tight with excitement and fear. They rushed to the shared hostel bathroom. It was already full. Boys were shouting, pushing, calling for turns at the mirror.

Aarav glanced at Vihan and whispered, "Looks like a fight scene already." Vihan smirked, "Just wait. The real drama hasn't even started." Water splashed. Someone complained loudly. Someone laughed. It was noisy, messy, and alive. In that chaos, friendships would begin. Secrets would be shared. Memories would be made in those tiled walls.

After getting ready, they walked to the dining hall. It was even louder. The smell of breakfast mixed with the chatter of students. Plates banged. Teachers and Warden tried to control the noise but failed. Everyone clung to their routines, trying to feel normal on a day that didn't feel normal at all.

Aarav and Vihan sat together, not talking much. They watched everything around them - the noise, the energy, the nervous excitement in every child's eyes.

"This is crazy," Aarav said softly.

Vihan nodded, "Yeah... but it feels like we're starting something big."

Aarav smiled. Vihan smiled back.

The orchestra of their new life had begun.

The First Day, The Last Bench

Aarav and Vihan walked toward the academic block, their school bags hanging from their shoulders. The tall building stood before them like a new world. Aarav felt both excited and scared. He whispered to Vihan, "Do you think it will be good?"

Vihan smiled a little. "We'll find out soon."

At the staircase, they stopped. A teacher was standing there, calling out instructions.

"Aarav, Classroom 3. Vihan, Classroom 4."

Both brothers looked at each other in surprise. They had assumed they would be together. Aarav's heart dropped a little, and Vihan could see it.

Vihan patted his shoulder. "Don't worry. We'll meet after class."

Aarav nodded quietly and walked toward Classroom 3 as he is the 3rd grade student.

He took a deep breath before entering. His stomach tightened. The room was full – many students, many strange faces. It felt huge, loud, and full of unknown stories.

Aarav thought, *Will I fit in here? Will I make friends? Will this place ever feel like home?*

His eyes fell on the blackboard. It was clean and empty, like a page waiting to be written on. Above it was a small green board with three names written in chalk. Aarav didn't know what they meant, but something told him that those names would matter later.

Rows of long iron benches filled the room - three students to a seat. Aarav prayed silently that he wouldn't have to sit next to a girl. Not because he didn't like them… but talking to them felt like solving a math problem with no formula.

He found a place in the middle row, where most boys were sitting. The classroom had already divided on its own—boys on one side, girls on another. That gave him a small sense of relief.

As he sat down, Aarav felt his heart slow a little. The noise of the classroom, the smell of chalk, the sound of students talking - it all blended together. It still felt strange, but it also felt like the beginning of something important.

Far down the hall, Vihan sat in Classroom 4 as he is the 4th grade student, probably feeling the same mix of fear and excitement.

Aarav whispered to himself, "Day One… let's begin."

A Quiet Start in the Back Row

Aarav slipped into a seat in the back middle row and let out a small breath of relief.

"Good spot," he whispered to himself. Close enough to listen, but far enough to stay unnoticed. He liked it that way. From here, he could watch everything without anyone watching him.

The classroom felt new in every way - new faces, new voices, new rules. The air was filled with excitement, laughter, and whispers. But one thing inside Aarav was the same - his shyness, especially around girls.

He looked around carefully. Most of the girls were talking among themselves. They looked confident, comfortable, like they already belonged here.

Aarav thought, *how do they talk so easily?*

Until now, he had only spoken freely with his mother and cousins. In front of girls he didn't know, his words always froze. His tongue felt heavy, and his mind blank.

Vihan wasn't beside him to joke or make him relax. He was alone here, at least for now.

Aarav rested his hands on the desk and whispered to himself, "It's okay… everyone starts somewhere."

He looked around again. Not everyone seemed confident. Some boys were nervous too, and some were also silent. That gave him a little comfort.

Aarav thought, *Friendship is like a seed. It needs time… and a little sunlight.*

The bell rang loudly, and the classroom fell quiet.

Aarav sat up straight.

"Day one," he murmured, "let's see how it goes."

The First Day Puzzle

The day moved forward like a puzzle. Every hour felt like a new piece - some full of curiosity, some full of fear, and some full of discovery. Aarav sat quietly, watching everyone around him. In his mind, he slowly started grouping his classmates.

He whispered to himself, "Hmm... maybe friends... maybe trouble... maybe just background."

He didn't know who would become important in his life, but he had a strange feeling that some faces in that room would remain in his story forever.

When the lessons began, Aarav's focus shifted to the teachers. Without planning to, he started studying them - not in a judging way, but with a sense of respect.

He thought, *this one explains well... this one tells stories... this one really loves teaching.*

Some teachers spoke with passion, some taught with patience, and some made even boring lessons feel interesting. Aarav knew those teachers would stay in his heart and memory.

By the end of the day, Aarav still didn't have all the answers he wanted. He didn't know who his friends would be, what challenges he would face, or how this new world would change him.

But he knew one thing for sure - this was not just the start of another school year.

This was the beginning of a new chapter, one that would need bravery, patience, and growth.

As he packed his bag, Vihan met him in the corridor.

"How was your first day?" Vihan asked.

Aarav smiled lightly. "Different... but good. I think the real story starts now."

Vihan laughed softly. "Then buckle up."

Aarav nodded, feeling stronger than before. The curtain had lifted. The chapter had begun.

Chapter:3
A Tale of Two Classes

In every school, there are two kinds of classes - some feel safe and calm, and others feel like a battlefield. For Aarav, the difference was clear as day.

The Battlefield: Hindi Class

Hindi class was war.

Under the sharp eyes of Ms. Sravya, every student sat stiff and silent. She was strict, famous for her loud scolding and her iron scale. The sound of it hitting the desk was enough to make hearts stop. Homework wasn't homework - it was survival.

Aarav already struggled with Hindi. Grammar confused him, vocabulary slipped from his memory, and reading felt slow and painful. But in this class, his fear didn't let him think. Every tick of the clock felt like a countdown to trouble.

He stared at his textbook, praying not to be called.

A boy next to him whispered, "Bro… I forgot my homework."

Aarav looked at him with wide eyes. "God help you," he whispered back.

But the teacher had heard the whisper.

"Both of you, stand up!" she barked.

Aarav's heart dropped. Even when he wasn't the one guilty, fear found him. Hindi was not just a subject - it was a red chalk warning written across his day.

The Sanctuary: English Class

But then came English class.

The moment Ms. Sindhu entered, the room felt different. Her voice was soft, her smile real. She didn't walk in with a scale… she walked in with stories.

"Today," she said, "we are going on an adventure."

And just like that, the whole class relaxed.

In English, Aarav didn't feel afraid. He felt alive. Stories made sense to him. Poems felt like songs. He didn't have to force words - they came on their own.

Once, while reading a story, Ms. Sindhu looked at him.

"Aarav, what do you think the character is feeling?"

Aarav spoke slowly but honestly. She listened carefully.

"Good," she said with a warm smile. "That is exactly right."

Aarav felt something he rarely felt in school - confidence.

English wasn't a subject anymore. It was freedom, a door to a world where he didn't have to be loud to be heard.

A Teacher Who Lit a Spark

Soon, writing became Aarav's secret voice.

He scribbled stories in the margins of his notebook.

He wrote what he couldn't say out loud.

His pen became his courage.

And Ms. Sindhu noticed.

She saw the spark in him before anyone else did. She appreciated his work, encouraged him, and believed in him even when he didn't believe in himself.

One day, she stood in front of the class.

"We need a class leader," she said.

"All of you know who deserves it."

She looked straight at Aarav.

"Aarav will be the leader."

The class clapped. Aarav felt his cheeks grow warm.

Vihan met him at lunch and grinned.

"Class leader, haan? Great start, bro."

Aarav laughed shyly. "Let's hope I survive Hindi class tomorrow."

But not everyone was happy.

Some students whispered.

Some stared.

Envy had entered the story.

Aarav didn't know it yet, but leadership would come with challenges - tests far tougher than grammar worksheets.

The battlefield was just beginning.

The Rivalry Begins

Aarav's success did not make everyone happy. Some classmates liked him and supported him. But others felt jealous.

Among them was one girl - smart, confident, and determined not to come second to anyone.

One day in class, she whispered across the desk,

Girl: "So, Aarav… another full score today?"

Aarav looked up, a little shy but calm.

Aarav: "I just tried my best."

She gave a small smile, but her eyes showed something sharper.

Girl: "Good. Because I'm going to beat you next time."

From that moment, every class felt different.

When the teacher asked questions, they both answered—faster, smarter, louder.

Each essay became a challenge.

Each compliment from the teacher felt like another match point.

Aarav began to feel the pressure.

English was no longer just about stories and imagination.

It became a test - a daily battle to stay on top.

One evening, Aarav shared his feelings with Vihan during study hour.

Aarav: "I don't know why she's so angry with me."

Vihan smiled gently.

Vihan: "Maybe she's not angry. Maybe she just wants to prove she's as good as you."

Aarav sighed.

Aarav: "I just want to enjoy class again."

Vihan placed a hand on his shoulder.

Vihan: "Then you will. Just stay true to who you are."

But deep inside, Aarav could feel it -

A rivalry had begun.

A quiet storm was rising, and it was going to change everything, but not enough to break his confidence.

Chapter:4
Rivalry and Recognition

Chalk and Sparks

Every classroom has silent fights - battles that no one writes on the noticeboard but everyone can feel. Who is the GIRL not happy for Aarav's growth and recognition?

For Aarav, that battle had a name: Selena

Selena was the girls' class leader - confident, sharp, and always ready to prove herself.

Aarav had been chosen the overall leader.

On paper, they were equals.

In reality, every compliment, every glance, every word on the blackboard turned into a challenge.

Whenever Ms Sindhu praised Aarav's answers or essays, Selena's eyes tightened. She kept telling herself it was only about being the best.

But deep inside, she felt something else - envy she couldn't hide.

Chalk Wars

One morning, Selena rushed to the board and began writing the day's schedule.

Her handwriting curved beautifully.

Aarav walked in and paused.

She turned slightly, smirking.

Selena: "You're late today."

Aarav: *smiles softly* "Only by a minute."

He picked up the second chalk and wrote beside her work - bold, neat, and simple.

The prefects nearby whispered and grinned.

Boy: "Today's winner? Aarav, I think."

Girl: "No way. Selena's handwriting is prettier."

For most students, it was funny.

For Aarav and Selena, it was serious.

The next day was the same.

Then the next.

A silent competition—no trophies, no announcements, but a fight that pushed both of them harder.

A Different Kind of Quiet

But life isn't only rivalry.

In the middle of all this stood Zia - calm, soft-spoken, and kind.

She didn't run to the blackboard.

She didn't try to beat anyone.

One afternoon, Aarav sat beside her in the library.

She looked up and smiled.

Zia: “You look tired.”

Aarav: “Maybe… a little. Too much competition.”

Zia nodded gently.

Zia: “A class doesn’t need winners. It needs peace.”

Her words stayed with him.

He found himself watching her sometimes - not because she was loud, but because she wasn’t.

The Storm Builds

Still, competition has its own fire.

With every test, every duty, every word of praise, the heat between Aarav and Selena grew stronger.

Aarav never asked for rivalry - but it followed him.

Selena couldn’t walk away—not yet.

Two leaders.

Two dreams.

One classroom is slowly turning into a battleground.

And somewhere in that storm…

Hearts were beginning to change.

Chapter:5
The Beginning of a True Friendship.

A Thread Between Them

At first, Aarav and Zia lived in two different corners of the classroom.

Zia was always with her friends - laughing, chatting, filling the room with warm energy.

Aarav stayed quiet, sitting in the back, observing more than he spoke.

To him, Zia was just another student - kind, bright, but far from his little circle.

He never even thought of talking to her.

But sometimes, friendship begins in the smallest ways.

One morning in Math class, Zia's pencil rolled off her desk and stopped near Aarav's shoes.

Aarav blinked, unsure for a moment.

Then he bent down, picked it up, and placed it carefully on her desk.

Zia looked at him, surprised but smiling.

Zia: "Thanks."

Aarav: softly "It's okay."

Their eyes met for a heartbeat - quick, simple, but honest.

Nothing special.

Yet for Aarav, it felt like the first tiny thread tying them together.

A few days later, Ms. Sindhu made pairs for reading practice.

Aarav and Zia ended up together.

Aarav felt his stomach twist.

Zia looked a little nervous too.

They opened the book.

Aarav: "Umm… should I start?"

Zia: *smiling* "Let's take turns?"

They began reading.

The first lines sounded stiff.

Then Aarav misread a word.

Zia laughed softly.

Zia: "Say it again… this time slowly."

Aarav: *laughing too* "I promise I can read!"

The awkwardness cracked open.

Suddenly, mistakes felt funny.

Reading felt lighter.

By the end of the lesson, the silence between them felt different.

not strange, not scary…

just comfortable.

A small friendship had begun - quiet, simple, and real.

Little by Little

Their bond grew in tiny ways:

Zia asking Aarav for an extra sheet.

Aarav lending his eraser before she even asked.

Whispering answers during group work.

A shy smile when their eyes met.

Nothing big.

Nothing dramatic.

Just small, ordinary moments that slowly built trust.

The Quiet Glow of Friendship

One afternoon, as everyone ran outside to play, Zia walked past Aarav.

She slowed down, gave him a warm smile, and said -

Zia: "Come fast. Let's play too."

Not shy.

Just friendly and familiar.

Aarav smiled back, feeling something shift inside him.

This wasn't confusing.

This wasn't a crush.

This wasn't anything dramatic.

It was simple:

Zia was no longer just another classmate.

She was becoming a friend - someone who noticed him, understood him, and made him feel included.

They weren't best friends yet.

But they weren't strangers anymore.

They were somewhere in between - two kids slowly learning to trust each other, share moments, and build something steady.

And for Aarav, in all the noise and rivalry of school, that small glow of friendship was exactly what he needed.

A beginning.

A thread.

A true friendship taking shape.

Chapter:6
The Hostel Stories Unfolding

The Boys Who Made the Hostel Home.

Hostel life wasn't only about studying or following rules.

For Aarav, it was a tiny world filled with noise, laughter, secrets, fights, and memories that stuck to the heart.

And at the centre of that world were three boys:

Sampath, Akhil Sai, and Akhil.

All different.

All special.

All impossible to forget.

Sampath - The Innocent Comedian

Sampath was the kind of boy who could make anyone laugh - even when he didn't mean to.

He had big eyes full of innocence and a smile that always arrived too early or too late.

He said the funniest things without trying.

He did the funniest things without knowing.

Sampath's Midnight Doubt

It was past midnight.

Most boys in the dorm were snoring softly.

Only Aarav was half awake, staring at the ceiling and waiting for sleep to come.

Suddenly, he heard a small whisper from the bed beside him.

Sampath: "Aarav… Aarav… you awake?"

Aarav sighed.

He already knew that tone - soft, scared, and confused.

Aarav: "Yes, Sampath. What happened?"

There was a long pause.

Then a tiny voice said:

Sampath: "Aarav… did I just… pee on my bed?"

Aarav looked over.

Sampath was sitting up, his blanket held tightly around him, eyes wide with embarrassment.

Aarav: *gently* "Yes, you did."

Sampath nodded slowly, thinking hard.

Then, in the same serious voice, he whispered:

Sampath: "Okay… I have a doubt."

Aarav rubbed his eyes.

Aarav: "What doubt now?"

Sampath looked truly troubled, like he was asking the biggest question in the world.

Sampath: "Why do I do this every day?"

Aarav burst out laughing, covering his mouth.

Sampath was innocence wrapped in chaos.

Everyone loved him for it.

Akhil Sai - The Naughty One

Akhil Sai was the spark in the group—sharp, sarcastic, fast with jokes.

He could roast anyone within three seconds and still make them laugh.

He was the one who hid shoes, swapped water bottles, and whistled during study hours.

Akhil Sai: "Boys… today we escape from the evening study."

Aarav: "How?"

Akhil Sai: "Simple. Act like stomach pain. They can't prove it."

Five minutes later, he was caught, standing in front of the warden.

Warden: "Where is your stomach pain?"

Akhil Sai: "Madam… it ran away after seeing you."

The whole dorm erupted.

He got punished, of course.

But he laughed all the way through it.

Akhil Sai was trouble.

But he was the kind of trouble everyone wanted around.

Akhil - The Balanced One

Akhil was different - sometimes serious, sometimes the most fun, sometimes quietly planning mischief no one suspected.

He tried to act mature, but it never worked for long.

And somehow, somehow…

he always became the victim of the hostel's endless card games.

If they played cards, Akhil lost.

Every. Single. Time.

Akhil: "Bro, why do I always lose?"

Akhil Sai: "Because destiny hates you in cards."

Sampath: "Even I can win against you, Akhil!"

Akhil: "This is bullying. I will complain."

But he never complained.

He just laughed and played again - and lost again.

Don't worry, it's just a kind of normal game cards, not something which you're thinking. Haha…

Akhil was the glue in the group - steady, warm, and ready for anything.

Aarav's Little World

The four of them, together, turned the hostel into a home:

Sampath's accidental jokes

Akhil Sai's fearless mischief

Akhil's perfect mix of seriousness and fun

Aarav's quiet smile as he watched all of them

They fought.

They teased.

They shared secrets after lights-out.

They stole food from tiffin boxes.

They laughed until their stomachs hurt.

In a strange new world, these boys became Aarav's comfort—his team, his family, his story.

And he knew one thing:

Hostel life wouldn't have been the same without them.

Loved by Their Teachers

Aarav and his friends had one more thing in common - teachers loved them.

Aarav had a way with words that even he didn't fully understand. When he wrote, his thoughts flowed like water, clean and calm. Ms. Sindhu, the English teacher, noticed it first.

She would smile whenever Aarav raised his hand.

Ms. Sindhu: "Aarav, would you like to read your paragraph?"

Aarav: *with a smile* "Yes, ma'am."

And as he read, the whole class listened.

But his friends - Sampath, Akhil Sai, and Akhil - were stars of a different kind.

Ms. Suhana, the Maths teacher, adored them.

They solved problems even before others finished writing the question.

Ms. Suhana: "Akhil Sai, how did you do this so fast?"

Akhil Sai: "Ma'am… magic."

Sampath: "Ma'am, don't trust him. He copied from me."

Akhil: "Both of them copied from me, ma'am."

And the whole class burst into laughter.

Their numbers danced as easily as Aarav's words danced.

But what made their bond special was simple -

there was no jealousy.

Never once did Aarav feel smaller because his friends were good at maths.

Never once did they feel less because Aarav shined in English.

Strengths were celebrated.

Weaknesses were joked about.

And friendship always stood taller than pride.

Aarav: "You three are Maths toppers. How?"

Sampath: "Because God loves me more."

Akhil Sai: "Because I cheat better."

Akhil: "Because they don't think before talking."

They all laughed, the kind of laugh that fills a room, a heart, a memory.

To their teachers, they were stars.

To each other, they were home.

Morning Mischief

Mornings in the hostel were never calm.

If someone ever sold tickets for the daily drama, it would be for one show only -

The Boys vs. ***Ms. Sai Rani, the Warden.***

Every day started the same way.

Ms. Rani: "Wake up! Get ready! It's time! Move, boys!"

Her voice shot through the corridor like an alarm clock no one could escape.

Aarav and his friends, of course, had their own morning plan.

Blankets went over their heads.

Shoes were pushed under the bed.

Laughter was buried deep in their throats.

It was their secret game - hide-and-seek, played every sunrise.

Sampath was always the weakest link.

Sampath: *whispering loudly* "Aarav… she's coming!"

Aarav slapped his own forehead.

Aarav: "Whisper, Sampath! Whisper!"

But Sampath's innocent giggles kept bubbling out.

Akhil Sai held his stomach, tears in his eyes from trying not to laugh.

Akhil Sai: "If she finds us, it's your fault, Sampath!"

Sampath: "Why mine? I'm not even laughing!"

Which, of course, made them laugh more.

And then there was Akhil - half serious, half sleepy.

Akhil: "This is nonsense. Let's just wake up."

But he didn't move even an inch.

Outside, Ms. Rani's footsteps grew louder.

Aarav: "Shh! Not a sound… she's right there."

They froze.

Not breathing.

Not blinking.

One wrong move and the whole room would explode into chaos.

But that was the fun.

The thrill of being almost caught.

The joy of sharing that fear with the people you loved like brothers.

Those small moments before the day began -

they were worth more than breakfast, more than sleep.

For those few minutes, they weren't just hostel boys following rules.

They were children - wild, free, laughing, alive.

Nights of Whispered Worlds

If mornings were full of chaos, nights were something else - quiet, soft, almost magical.

When the hostel lights went off and the corridors turned silent, the boys' room came alive. They gathered on one bed, pulling a blanket over their heads. A small torch glowed underneath, lighting up their smiling faces.

Homework fear, Ms. Sravya's punishments, Ms. Rani's shouting - none of it mattered here. Not in their secret night world.

Sampath: *whispering loudly* "Tomorrow… I swear… we'll escape again."

His grin stretched from ear to ear.

Akhil Sai: "And I'll be the lookout!"

He puffed his chest even in the dark, making the others laugh.

Akhil: "You both are idiots."

He rolled his eyes, but his hidden smile said something else.

Akhil: "We should be studying instead."

Aarav: "Study in the morning, serious boy."

He nudged Akhil lightly.

Their laughter shook the bed, but they quickly pressed hands over their mouths so the warden wouldn't hear. Outside, the night was silent. Inside, four boys were building their own little world - a kingdom made of jokes, dreams, and promises spoken in whispers.

The Warmth of Belonging

As the torchlight flickered and sleep slowly wrapped around them, they spread across their beds. The whispers faded, the room softened, and silence returned.

Aarav lay still, looking at the ceiling, a small smile resting on his lips. Maybe hostel life wasn't just about rules, study hours, or fear of punishments. Maybe it was about this - these stolen moments, these midnight laughs, these boys who felt like family.

With that warm thought in his chest, he finally closed his eyes.

And the night carried him gently into dreams - dreams filled with friendship, safety, and the feeling of truly belonging.

Chapter:7
The Shadows of Fear & The Rising Anger

The Silence in Her Classroom

Classrooms are supposed to be noisy - full of laughter, questions, and small mistakes that help children learn.

But in Ms. Sravya's room, there was only silence.

Not the peaceful kind.

The heavy kind.

The kind that sits in the corners and makes every child hold their breath.

Her punishments were not simple scoldings. They were public shows - loud, sharp, meant to break confidence. The iron scale in her hand looked more like a weapon. Every student in the class had felt its sting.

The sound it made - crack! - cut through the air and cut through their hearts too.

Red lines burned on their palms long after the class ended. But the real pain wasn't on the skin. It was inside. It was the shame of being made small in front of everyone else.

Aarav's Breaking Point

Aarav knew this fear better than anyone.

Again and again, he found himself standing in front of the class, palms shaking, eyes lowered, waiting for the scale to strike. Every time it hit, his heart tightened. Every time it burned, his pride shrank.

Inside his mind, questions screamed:

"Is this learning?"

"Are we supposed to feel scared every day?"

But his lips stayed quiet. They always did.

At first, he tried to accept it.

At first, he told himself, *maybe this is how school works.*

But the more he watched, the more something changed inside him.

He saw the quiet boy who never raised his hand.

He saw the girl who wiped tears before anyone noticed.

He saw his own friends looking down at their desks, afraid to even breathe too loudly.

And something inside Aarav snapped - not loudly, not suddenly, but firmly.

This was no longer discipline.

This was fear.

And fear was killing their joy, their curiosity, their courage.

The Spark of Rebellion

Every day, the air felt heavier. Every lesson felt like a burden. But with that heaviness came something new - a growing fire in Aarav's heart.

Silence couldn't hold him forever.

Fear couldn't bend him forever.

He didn't know when it would happen.

He didn't know how.

But he knew one thing clearly:

This wouldn't go on forever.

One day, the anger inside him would speak.

One day, the fear would break.

One day, someone would stand up.

And deep inside Aarav…

the first spark had already been lit.

The fire was on its way.

Chapter:8
A Day of Reckoning

The 60th Morning

The 60th morning at boarding school *looked* like any other.

The sun was soft, the air was cool, and boys rushed around with half - tucked shirts and sleepy faces.

But as Aarav walked toward his classroom, something felt different - heavier.

The corridor was full of noise:

laughter bouncing off the walls,

notebooks flipping open,

friends teasing each other,

footsteps racing to beat the bell.

But for Aarav, it all felt far away.

Like he was walking through a tunnel where every sound reached him late.

Inside him, something was building.

A quiet storm.

A mix of too many things that had piled up over days and weeks.

Ms. Sravya's punishments.

The sharp pain of the scale.

The fear in everyone's eyes.

Selena's endless rivalry.

Every competition.

Every comparison.

Every moment he felt pushed, judged, cornered.

All of it pressed down on him now - on this morning.

As he walked, Aarav's chest felt tight, his steps slow, his breath uneven.

Akhil noticed first.

Akhil: "Hey… you, okay?"

Aarav: forcing a small smile "Yeah. Just tired."

But Akhil didn't look convinced.

Behind them, Sampath hurried over, almost tripping on his own shoelaces.

Sampath: "Aarav, why your face looks like you ate a lemon?"

Aarav: a soft laugh "Nothing like that."

Akhil Sai joined them, slinging an arm over Aarav's shoulder.

Akhil Sai: "Don't lie. We know when your brain is full."

Aarav looked at his three friends -

the silly one,

the serious one,

the mischievous one -

and his heart felt a little lighter.

But the storm didn't fade.

It stayed inside him, waiting.

The 60th morning had begun.

And something in the air whispered…

Today would not be ordinary.

The Sudden Disruption

By noon, the class was buzzing with noise.

Zia, Selena, and Jayani were laughing in their corner, sharing some silly joke.

The boys were arguing over crayons.

Everything felt normal - light, warm, safe.

Then the door creaked.

Ms. Sravya stepped in.

Her presence sucked the air out of the room.

"An extra Hindi class," she said, her voice sharp.

The words hit the class like a stone dropped in water.

The laughter stopped.

Voices died.

Heads bent down.

Aarav felt his heart drop to his stomach.

He remembered -

He hadn't done the Hindi assignment.

His fingers tightened on his notebook

as Ms. Sravya's eyes moved from one row

to the next

to the next…

And then stopped on him.

"Aarav," she said, loud enough for everyone to hear.

"Have you completed your assignment?"

The class went still.

Every head turned toward him.

Two choices flashed through his mind:

lie and get caught later…

or tell the truth and face the pain.

He swallowed.

His voice was small, but steady.

"No, ma'am."

The silence in the room grew heavier.

"Come forward," she ordered.

Aarav stood.

His legs felt weak, but he walked anyway.

She lifted the iron scale.

Everyone held their breath.

The strike landed.

A sharp crack.

Heat shot through his palm like fire.

Aarav shut his eyes for a second -

but he didn't cry.

Not today.

He walked back slowly, hand burning, face blank.

Around him, his classmates sat stiff and scared, secretly praying she wouldn't call their names next.

An Unexpected Arrival

What Aarav didn't know was that fate had already changed direction.

His father had come to school that day.

For weeks, he had listened to Aarav's quiet voice over phone calls -

talking about punishments,

about fear,

about pain he didn't deserve.

But hearing was one thing.

Seeing was another.

The moment he saw the red, swollen marks on Aarav's hands, something snapped inside him.

Anger - hot, sharp, protective—rose like fire.

He marched straight to the principal's office.

No more silence.

No more excuses.

Today, someone would answer for hurting his child.

Summoned to the Principal

Back in class, Aarav sat staring at the angry red line on his palm, fighting back the ache.

Then the floor boy walked in.

"Aarav, you are called to the principal's office."

A wave of whispers rolled through the classroom.

Before the noise could settle, the boy continued:

"Ms. Sravya, you are also requested."

This time, the whispering exploded.

Eyes widened.

Chins lifted.

Something was happening - something big.

For the first time, a small hope lit up in the children's eyes.

Maybe… maybe the fear that ruled their classroom was finally about to break.

The Day Everything Changed.

Inside the principal's office, the air felt tight.

Ms. Rekha sat straight behind her desk, her face calm but serious.

Aarav's father leaned forward in his chair, his hands clenched, anger sitting right behind his eyes.

The door opened slowly.

Ms. Sravya stepped in.

Her usual confidence was gone. She looked unsure, almost scared. This was not her classroom. This was not a place where she could shout or threaten. Here, she was just a teacher being asked to answer for what she had done.

Ms. Rekha turned to Aarav.

"Aarav," she asked gently, "is she the one? The one who hurt you?"

Aarav looked at Ms. Sravya.

At the scale marks still burning on his hand.

At the memories of fear in his classmates' eyes.

He took a small breath.

"Yes, ma'am," he said softly.

"Not just me. She punishes the whole class."

His voice was quiet, but the truth in it shook the room.

Aarav's father spoke next. His voice was low, but every word carried fire.

"Is this how you teach? By beating children? By making them afraid to learn? Afraid even to breathe?"

Ms. Sravya opened her mouth, but no words came.

Her throat tightened.

Her eyes filled with tears.

For the first time, she had no scale, no loud voice, no power.

Only shame.

Ms. Rekha let the silence stretch for a moment before speaking.

"A formal complaint will be filed," she said firmly.

"This ends today."

No one argued.

There was nothing left to say.

Afterwards

Ms. Sravya walked out of the office slowly, her face pale, her steps unsteady.

The woman who used to throw fear like stones now looked like someone crushed under her own choices.

She didn't return to class that day.

When Aarav walked back into the room, every head turned.

Whispers rushed around him like wind.

"What happened?"

"Did she get in trouble?"

"Is she gone?"

For the first time in a long time, their voices weren't scared.

They were hopeful.

The iron scale was gone.

The fear was cracked.

Zia looked at Aarav with soft surprise - like she had never really seen him before.

Aarav smiled back - small, but true.

He hadn't brought justice just for himself.

He had done it for everyone sitting in that room.

The Whisper of Change

Something shifted that day.

The classroom felt lighter, brighter - almost like it could breathe again.

Children sat up straighter, not out of fear but out of relief.

It didn't mean school suddenly became easy.

Exams were still near.

Rivalries still existed.

Problems didn't disappear.

But one thing changed forever -

Aarav had found his courage.

And courage, once found, does not leave.

It only grows.

This was not the end of his story.

This was the beginning of who he was meant to become.

Chapter:9
When the Washroom Became a Playground

Some memories are so silly, so over-the-top, that they feel like made-up stories. But for Aarav and his hostel brothers, the bathroom memories were real - real like scraped knees, late-night talks, and shared secrets before sleep. In their boarding school life, the bathroom wasn't just a place with taps and buckets. It was a place where they laughed, fought, teased each other, and created moments they would never forget. It was their small, noisy world of comedy, chaos, and mischief - where childhood truly lived.

The Secret Fort of the Hostel Boys

Every floor of the hostel had a huge bathroom. Long lines of basins, rows of showers, big echoing cubicles, and a wide wash area that looked more like a stadium than a bathroom. With all the shining taps, it even felt like a place lit by tiny floodlights.

For Aarav and his friends, this wasn't just a bathroom.

It was their secret fort.

Whenever a boring class - especially Hindi period - was about to start, the boys quietly slipped away. The moment they pushed the bathroom door open, they felt safe. The warm steam, the soft echoes, the smell of soap - everything made the place feel like their own little world.

Warden Ms. Rani was the only threat. She had sharp eyes and a voice that could shake the whole corridor. She searched for them like a hunter.

"Where are those boys?" she would shout. But the bathroom was their fortress. Hidden behind the steam, behind their whispers and laughter, they felt invisible. Of course, the peace didn't last forever. Sometimes, Ms. Rani would barge inside, her steps loud and angry.

"There you are! Out! Now!" she yelled.

The boys ran out, pretending to be scared but secretly smiling. Because even if they got caught, the fun was already theirs. For a few precious minutes, they had escaped school, rules, and everything else.

In that bathroom, they weren't just students.

They were free.

The Great Water Fight

Mornings in the hostel bathroom were never ordinary. What began as a simple routine - soap, scrub, rinse - quickly turned into chaos.

Buckets weren't just buckets. They were cannons. Mugs weren't for water - they were grenades. The wet, slippery tiles became a skating rink of madness.

Aarav would tiptoe, eyes sparkling with mischief, and dump a bucket of icy water over a friend. Akhil Sai would sneak behind someone, pushing their head into a tub of frothy soap. The victim would pop up, spluttering, bubbles in his eyes, laughing through the chaos.

The boldest move? Climbing the cubicle partition to pour water from above on anyone who thought they were safe inside. The shocked yell that followed was music to their ears.

Showers rattled. Latches banged. Doors shook. Boys locked each other in, freed each other, and slid across the soapy floor like champions in a game only they understood.

And through it all, one sound ruled: laughter - wild, loud, and free, echoing off cold, tiled walls.

For a few minutes every morning, the bathroom wasn't just a place to clean up. It was a battlefield, a playground, and a kingdom all at once.

More Than Mischief

To anyone else, it might have looked like chaos - pure, wild madness. But to Aarav, it was something deeper. These weren't just pranks. Every splash of water, every playful shove, every sneaky giggle built something bigger.

It was trust.

It was friendship.

It was joy that didn't care about rules or punishments.

By the time they finally stumbled out, soaking wet, out of breath from laughter and trembling from the warden's scolding, they weren't just boys getting ready for class. They were a team, carrying shared secrets in every dripping uniform and every mischievous grin.

The hostel walls had seen it all - the quiet conspiracies, the reckless laughter, the small acts of rebellion. And if those walls could speak, they'd tell this story: even in the smallest, most ordinary corners, Aarav, and his friends found magic. They had turned a simple bathroom into a cinema of memories - memories that would last a lifetime.

Chapter: 10
April Fools in the Hostel

Evenings in the hostel always had a special energy. After a long day of classes, the boys were alive with stories, secrets, and tiny schemes. Laughter bounced off the walls, whispers travelled across beds, and every little mischief felt bigger than life.

On one such evening, Aarav sat on his bed, a spark in his eyes. He had an idea - bold, crazy, and just a little bit dangerous.

"This... this will make me a legend," he whispered to himself, grinning.

The Spark of an Idea

A few days ago, Aarav had a nasty accident. A sharp iron rod had cut into his leg, deep enough to make him wince with every step. The wound sent him straight to a hospital, four or five kilometres away. He got stitched up and was sent back under strict supervision.

But pain has a strange way of sparking imagination. That night, lying in bed with his leg aching, Aarav's mind wandered. A new movie had just come out - the one every boy in the hostel was desperate to see.

What if… he thought, I tell them I sneaked into the cinema after the hospital?

The thought made him grin. He imagined the looks on his friends' faces - the wide eyes, the nonstop questions, the disbelief. It was too tempting to ignore.

And just like that, Aarav's prank was born.

The Perfect Lie

By nightfall, Aarav's story was ready - polished and perfect. Sitting cross-legged with his roommates, he leaned in and began.

"I went straight into the cinema," he said, eyes wide with mock excitement. "The hall was huge, lights dim, the crowd crazy! And then this one scene - you wouldn't believe it…"

He described the movie as if he had been there, added a few made-up dramatic bits, and spoke with such conviction that even Sampath, Akhil Sai, and Akhil hung on every word.

The boys' jaws dropped. Some groaned in envy. "Why weren't we there?!" one whispered. Others begged for spoilers. Aarav smirked behind his serious face. For once, he wasn't just the boy with stitches - he was the cleverest trickster in the hostel.

That night, as he snuggled under his blanket, he thought, *let them stew in jealousy tonight. Tomorrow, I'll reveal the truth. No harm done.*

The Twist of Fate

But hostel life has its own plans.

At dawn, curiosity got the better of his friends. Tiptoeing to the medical staff, they asked casually, "Sir… after the hospital… did Aarav really go to the movie?"

The staff blinked, confused. "Movie? What nonsense! We went straight to the hospital and straight back."

Aarav's flawless story collapsed in an instant. The boys' shock quickly turned into laughter. Their envy became delight. They had been fooled - but now, the prank stage was theirs.

Tables Turned

Back in the dorm, Aarav still slept, dreaming of his own cleverness. His friends huddled, whispering and grinning.

"Wake him up?" Sampath asked.

"Not yet," Akhil Sai smirked. "Let's make him sweat first."

They plotted in silence. If Aarav thought he could outsmart them, they were ready to remind him that in the hostel, every prank had a sequel.

The Secret Plan

In the shadows, the mission began.

"He tricked us," Sampath whispered, eyes gleaming. "Now it's our turn."

"Bathroom," Akhil Sai grinned. "Let's baptize him properly."

They lifted Aarav from his bed, trying not to laugh, and carried him down the corridor. The hostel bathroom awaited - shiny tiles, lined-up showers, and buckets ready like soldiers.

They placed Aarav under a shower tap, his body limp with sleep.

The Wake-Up Call

Click. A sudden gush of icy water slammed over Aarav's head. His eyes shot open. SPLASH! SPLASH! - mugs and buckets rained down.

"What - what's happening?!" Aarav sputtered, spluttering, dripping.

"This is for your fake movie story! For fooling us!" his friends shouted, laughing so hard they could barely aim.

Aarav thrashed, shouted, and splashed back. Soon, his protests turned into giggles, then full-blown laughter. The punishment had become a festival.

The Big Reveal

Finally, soaked and shivering, Aarav raised his hands.

"Stop! Stop! You win! It was all an **April Fool's prank**! You fell for it!"

For a moment, silence. Then - BOOM! Water flew again, laughter bouncing off the walls. Boys rolled on the wet floor, faces aching from smiling.

A Healing in Disguise

When the chaos ended, the bathroom looked like a pool. Clothes stuck to skin, hair dripping, breathless giggles everywhere. Aarav leaned against the wet wall, heart light. His leg no longer hurt. His pride no longer weighed him down.

Around him, his friends—his brothers in laughter, rivals in pranks, family in the hostel - grinned.

Aarav whispered to himself, smiling:

"This… this is why hostel life is the best."

Chapter: 11
The Lizard and The Ghost

Nightmares of the Hostel.

The dorm stretched long, fifteen beds lined up like soldiers on parade. Night wrapped the room in heavy quiet, broken only by snores, sighs, and the occasional mumble of dreams. But Aarav lay wide awake, staring at the ceiling like a soldier on watch.

Above him, lizards scuttled along the wall. Tiny claws scratched the plaster, a sharp "tik-tik" echoing like a drumbeat of doom. Aarav gripped his blanket tighter, eyes following every jump, every sprint.

"Why me?" he whispered under his breath. "Out of all the beds... mine has to be next to the lizard highway. Look at them! Doing push-ups, running marathons, throwing a disco above my head!"

Another sharp "tik-tik." Aarav yelped, blanket covering his face.

"One day," he muttered, "one of them will drop straight on my face... and that's the day I quit hostel life."

Across the room, his friends snored peacefully, completely unaware of his struggle. Aarav glared at them.

"Of course… you all sleep like babies. To you, lizards are pets. To me - they're dinosaurs with gym memberships."

Operation Bed Swap

Aarav couldn't take it anymore. The lizard disco above his head was relentless. Quietly, he slipped off his bed, tiptoeing across the cold floor.

He crouched by Sampath's bed and nudged him.

"Sampath… shift a little. I can't sleep under that lizard disco anymore."

Sampath groaned, muffling his words under the blanket. "No chance, bro. Remember last week? You kicked me three times in your sleep. Go cuddle with your lizard."

Aarav sighed and padded to Akhil Sai's bed. He tried lying down, but the bed was too small. One false move, and he nearly rolled off. Frustrated, he gave up, cheeks red with exasperation.

Finally, with dramatic flair, he barged into Vihan's room and collapsed onto his bed.

"Brother! Save me. Lizards have taken over my wall."

Vihan hugged his blanket like a shield, whispering nervously, "And ghosts have taken over my bathroom corridor. Great. Together, we're the bravest cowards in this hostel."

The two huddled under the same blanket, shivering, whispering, their imaginations fueling each other's fears. Every creak in the corridor, every shadow on the wall became a shared adventure - or a shared horror.

In that small, trembling cocoon, Aarav realized something: even in terror, even under imaginary invasions, the comfort of a friend made the night almost bearable.

The Night Corridor Horror

Hours later, Aarav nudged Vihan.

"Bro… I need to go to the bathroom."

Vihan froze, eyes wide. "No way. The ghosts are on night duty. You go alone."

"Ghosts?! What about the lizards in the corridor?! I'm not dying today."

"Fine. We'll go together. But if a ghost grabs me, I'm using you as a shield."

"And if a lizard falls, I'm sacrificing you first," Aarav whispered, eyes darting around.

Clutching each other like they were entering a haunted mansion, the two crept into the corridor. A tube light flickered above, casting long, twitching shadows on the walls. Every creak of the floor sounded like footsteps of monsters.

Suddenly, a loud bang echoed - the bathroom door slammed in the wind.

Both screamed in unison:

"AAAAAAAAH!"

Then silence. Realization dawned. It was only the wind.

Still trembling, they tiptoed into the bathroom, moving like thieves caught mid-crime. Every tap glinting in the faint light, every shadow in the corner, seemed ready to spring to life. Yet, despite the fear, a spark of laughter threatened to break out—they were in this together.

Even in the dark, with ghosts imagined and lizards imagined bigger than life, the boys found courage… and fun.

The Hostel Comedy Club

Morning spilled into the dorm, bright and teasing. Aarav yawned, rubbing his eyes, still half-asleep.

"Careful, Aarav!" Akhil Sai shouted, pointing. "There's a lizard on your shoulder!"

Aarav jumped three feet, flailing wildly. He swatted at nothing, shrieking, while the dorm erupted in laughter.

Sampath, barely holding back his grin, nudged Vihan. "And Vihan… last night, the ghost in the corridor said hi to me. Wants to meet you tonight."

Vihan's eyes went wide. He dove under his blanket like it was a life raft.

The boys howled. Their laughter bounced off the walls, rolling through the room like music. Every exaggerated squeal, every jump, every snicker became part of the morning show.

What had been a night of lizards, flickering lights, and imagined ghosts had transformed into a morning of joy. For Aarav and Vihan, their fears had become legends - stories that would echo in the hostel for months, retold with laughter and embellishment.

Even the small, ordinary dorm felt like a stage that morning, and the boys - heroes of their own little comedy club - couldn't stop grinning.

Chapter: 12

The Evening That Never Ended: A Movie called "ALLADDIN"

Movie probably called as "ALLADDIN ADBUTHA DEEPAM"

Movie evenings were like festivals in the hostel. The moment the warden announced it, the whole building lit up with cheers. But no one was happier than Aarav. For him, a movie evening meant two precious things - time with his friends and a break from the long, strict study hours.

"Movie today! Finally!" Aarav whispered to Sampath, almost jumping.

Sampath laughed. "Bro, calm down. It's not like they're taking us to a theatre."

Aarav grinned. "Still… a movie is a movie!"

The so-called "movie hall" was just the library room with a big projector. The chairs were mismatched, some squeaky, some too big, some too small - but none of that mattered. Everyone squeezed in with excitement, waiting to find out which movie the teachers had chosen this time.

No one ever knew beforehand.

The teachers planned everything in secret, like it was a surprise gift.

Finally, the lights dimmed. The projector flickered on.

A voice whispered from the front,

"Today, we will watch Allauddin Adbutha Dweepam."

A soft wave of excitement ran through the room.

"Ayyoo! That animation movie? I heard it's beautiful," Akhil said.

"Love story, no?" Vihan smirked.

Aarav nodded shyly. "But it's different… it feels magical."

As the movie started, the room fell silent. The colours, the music, the dreamy island, and the sweet bond between the boy and the girl - everything pulled the children into a world far away from homework, tests, and hostel life.

Aarav was lost in it.

His eyes were wide, glowing with curiosity.

His heart felt warm, almost floating.

"This is so good…" he whispered.

"Shhh," Sampath elbowed him. "Let me watch."

But right when the story was reaching its most beautiful part - right when the boy and girl were about to speak their hearts - the door slammed open.

The principal walked in with a serious face.

"Students," he announced, "movie time is over. Everyone returns to study hours."

The projector clicked off.

The room fell into stunned silence.

“What? Already?” someone whispered.

“No, sir… please… five more minutes…” another student begged.

But rules were rules.

The students stood slowly, their faces heavy.

Aarav didn’t move. His eyes were stuck on the blank wall where the movie had just played.

“Bro, come,” Sampath said softly.

Aarav swallowed hard. “But… what happened to them? Did they meet again? Did they fall in love? Why did they stop it now?”

“No idea,” Vihan sighed. “Let’s go.”

But Aarav couldn’t forget.

Even during study hour, his pencil stayed still.

His mind replayed the movie, scene by scene.

That night, as he lay in bed, he whispered into the dark,

“I want to know the ending… I really want to know.”

That unfinished love story stayed with him.

Years passed.

Aarav grew up.

He became busy, older, stronger.

But even in his early 20s, he still hadn’t watched that movie again.

Not because he couldn’t… but because life kept moving, and time kept slipping away.

Somewhere inside him, the 7-year-old boy still waited - waiting to return to that tiny library room, sit between his friends, and finally see how the story ended.

And maybe, someday, he would.

Because some evenings don't end when the lights go out.

Some evenings stay alive in the heart forever.

Chapter: 13
When the Years Changed Them.

Days passed.

Months slipped away.

And before they even realised it, Aarav was now in 5th grade, and Vihan had stepped into 6th.

They were still the same boys in many ways - playful, noisy, full of dreams.

But hostel life had shaped them, sharpened them, softened them.

It taught them what missing someone feels like.

What it means to lose a friend, and what it means to find a new one.

How rivalry can turn into respect.

How pure friendship can feel like family.

And how love, in its small silent ways, can grow even in the corner of a classroom.

Aarav and Vihan had given their best in the previous year's exams. And now, with new classes, new books, and new pressure, they were getting ready to do it all over again.

One evening, as they sat on the corridor steps, Aarav tied his shoelace and sighed.

"Vihan… exams are coming again. I don't know why, but I feel nervous this time."

Vihan nudged him with his shoulder.

"Because you think too much, hero. Just study. You always do well."

Aarav looked down at his hands. "I left home for this… for study, for a better future. Amma and Nanna trust me so much. I don't want to fail them."

Vihan smiled softly. "You won't. You've never given up, even when things were tough. You're stronger than you know."

Aarav looked at him, grateful. "And you… you're always there."

"Of course," Vihan replied. "Brothers, no?"

The fact of the matter is that no one can understand you better than your own brother. In a place where parents are invisible, the two boys were growing in their own ways while learning so many things.

Life inside the hostel's four walls was still noisy - boys running, shouting, laughing, fighting over snacks, hiding storybooks under pillows, and secretly planning late-night talks.

But underneath the laughter, every boy was carrying something - dreams, fears, memories of home.

And Aarav carried all of it too.

Every night before he slept, he thought of his father's calm voice, his mother's warm touch.

He whispered to himself, "Do well. Make them proud."

He had stood strong all these years - through homesickness, exams, fights, punishment, friendships, heartbreaks, victories.

Like a small rock learning to survive the storm.

Now, standing at the edge of another exam season, Aarav felt something different -

a quiet courage in his chest.

A belief that he was no longer the little boy who arrived with fear in his eyes.

On the last night before the exams began, Vihan looked at him and asked,

"Ready?"

Aarav nodded slowly. "Yes. One last exam... one last chance to give everything."

And together, under the dim hostel corridor light, the two brothers walked back to their rooms -

prepared, hopeful, and stronger than ever.

Chapter: 14
The Green Board Dreams.

The Battle for the Board.

Final exam season had arrived like a quiet storm. The hostel, once bursting with laughter and chaos, now hummed with focus. Corridors echoed with the soft rustle of papers, the scratch of pens, and the occasional whisper. Tube lights cast a dim glow over the late-night warriors hunched over their desks.

For Aarav, these exams were more than numbers. They were a chance to prove himself, a chance to turn effort into glory. His eyes often drifted to the classroom's green board - the sacred board of pride - where the top three scorers' names would be written in bright white chalk.

Every day, he imagined it: **Aarav** - etched there, celebrated, remembered. Not just in chalk, but in memory, in laughter shared, in quiet respect.

But dreams were never simple. Especially when Mathematics loomed, like a stubborn shadow, mocking his every move. Numbers twisted and tangled on the page, teasing him with their complexity.

Still, this time, it felt different. Aarav's heart thrummed with determination. Every late-night scribble, every whispered calculation, every frustrated sigh was a step closer. He wasn't just fighting for grades - he was fighting for himself.

This was more than exams. This was his battle for the board.

The Circle of Friends

Aarav wasn't facing the exams alone. Around him stood his friends, a circle of trust turned study squad. Sampath, Akhil Sai, and Akhil - each quick with numbers - turned confusing sums into laughs, tricky formulas into small stories, and impossible problems into riddles he could finally solve.

And then there was Zia. Calm, patient, steady - like a lighthouse in the storm of Aarav's panic. She explained the hardest questions as if they were puzzles meant to be fun. Side by side, sharing notes, whispering answers, giggling at silly mistakes - they weren't just solving math. They were building trust, patience, and quiet friendship.

Her presence gave him strength, a hand guiding him through the chaos. With every solved problem, every shared laugh, the group felt like more than friends - they were a team, holding each other up.

Their little study sessions spread like warmth through the class. Rivalries faded, fear eased, and slowly, the challenge of exams became something they faced together. It wasn't just about marks anymore. It was about surviving, learning, and growing as one.

Selena's Silent Storm

Not everyone was happy with this new circle of friends.

Selena watched from afar, her chest tightening with every shared notebook, every quiet laugh between Zia and Aarav. Zia was her best friend, Aarav her rival. Seeing them connect felt like a betrayal. Every smile Zia gave him felt like a thorn. Every whispered explanation felt like a crack in her own bond with Zia.

For Aarav, it was just studying, nothing more. But for Selena, it was a battle - loyalty against rivalry, friendship against envy. A quiet storm had begun inside her, small but dangerous, threatening to change everything.

Between Fun and Focus

Hostel life had its own rhythm, one that never stopped. One moment, chalk flew like bullets during late-night revisions; the next, silence reigned as mock tests began. Pages rustled, pencils scratched, and trunks quietly opened to reveal midnight snacks - fuel for both laughter and study.

The countdown ticked: ten days... nine... eight. Each number pressed tension into the air. Yet beneath it all, friendships grew stronger. Every silly joke, every serious correction, every stolen biscuit became part of a grand, unforgettable montage - a mix of chaos, learning, and the joy of being together.

Aarav's Silent Promise to his family and himself

For Aarav, every solved sum was more than a number. It was a promise to himself - a vow that this time, he wouldn't be the boy who almost made it. This time, he would reach the green board - not for fame, not for pride, but for proof. Proof that he could.

Somewhere in his heart, he knew Zia's calm guidance, his friends' stubborn support, and his own burning determination might finally carry him there.

The exams ahead weren't just a test of knowledge. They were a test of friendship, rivalry, loyalty, and dreams.

And the real results, Aarav felt, would last far longer than marks on a paper.

Chapter: 15

The Last Day on the Green Board

The morning of results dawned like a slow-motion opening scene - nervous footsteps echoing down the corridors, whispers floating through the air, hands fidgeting with pens, notebooks, and sleeves. The classroom wasn't just a room anymore; it was a stage where destinies would be written in chalk.

Everywhere, one question buzzed like electricity: Who will make it to the Green Board?

For Aarav, time stretched painfully thin. His friends cracked nervous jokes, but their own eyes betrayed the storm within. Zia sat poised, calm as a still lake, while Selena's restless shifting gave her away - her gaze locked on the empty board like a gambler waiting for the last card. Then, with a screech of chalk, the silence broke.

1st Place - Zia

2nd Place - Jayani

3rd Place - Aarav

The room erupted. Cheers spilled out like a flood, boys clapping, friends slapping Aarav's back as if they had won alongside him. Zia's serene face glowed now with unguarded joy, her composure finally cracking into a smile of triumph. Even shy Jayani, who usually blended into the background, sat straighter, her cheeks pink with pride.

But amidst the celebration, one silence cut sharper than the noise.

Selena. Fourth place. So close - yet just a breath away from the board. She stared at the names, her jaw tightening, as though sheer will could rearrange them. But chalk, unlike dreams, does not bend.

The Moment of Silence

As applause roared, Aarav did something unexpected. He slipped away from the group's laughter and walked toward Selena. His steps were slow, deliberate - not of a victor, but of someone carrying an unspoken truth.

His voice, when it came, was steady and soft.

"Congratulations."

Selena blinked, startled. She had braced for teasing, maybe even smugness. But what she found instead was a calm, almost disarming gentleness.

Before she could respond, Aarav continued.

"Forget everything," he said, his words flowing like lines rehearsed in his heart a hundred times.

From tomorrow, I am not your classmate.

From tomorrow, I am not your enemy.

From tomorrow, I won't even be your competitor.

Because from tomorrow… I won't be your schoolmate anymore.

His words feel heavy, rippling through the room. The chatter dimmed; even the air seemed to hold its breath.

Aarav's eyes softened as he added, "You've been my strongest competitor, my sweetest enemy, and maybe, without knowing, one of my greatest teachers. I don't want to leave remembering you with anger."

The classroom that had moments ago shaken with laughter now sank into silence. A few lowered their eyes. Some blinked back unexpected tears. Even Zia, calm and composed as ever, felt her heart twist at the honesty laid bare.

And Selena - her fortress of rivalry, brick by brick, suddenly cracked.

The Farewell That Changed Everything

Selena throat tightened. Her eyes stung. She turned away quickly, fighting the tears that betrayed her. But Aarav didn't wait for her reply. He simply smiled - a small, knowing smile - nodded once, and walked back to his friends.

For the first time, Selena didn't see Aarav as the boy who defeated her. She saw him for what he truly was: someone who respected her enough to let rivalry end with kindness.

That day, the Green Board carried more than three names.

It carried lessons - about ambition, about friendship, about rivalry, and about parting with grace.

The Whisper of Change

When Aarav stepped out of the classroom for the last time, he didn't turn back. But the silence he left behind lingered. The laughter quieted. The tears some fought to hide said more than words ever could.

For some, he was the competitor who pushed them higher.

For some, he was the friend who filled hostel life with laughter.

For Selena, he would always remain the rival who walked away with respect.

And for Aarav himself, the Green Board had given him more than a rank.

It had given him a memory carved deep into the walls of that classroom, etched forever in the hearts that had shared the journey with him.

He hadn't just earned a place on the Green Board.

He had earned a place in stories, in friendships, in memories that would outlast chalk and time itself.

Before I Close This Part.

Author Closing Note.

Every time I listened to my heart, it reminded me of one truth **– it was never easy to live so far from my parents at such a young age.**

Sometimes I asked myself,

why did this happen?

And sometimes I wondered, why shouldn't it?

What started as confusion slowly turned into pain, and then into a quiet fear… a fear of losing something precious.

I was just a child, but I felt it all.

I felt the weight of everything I had left behind at home - my loving parents, and most of all, my sister.

With her, I hardly had a real childhood.

From being a hosteller from **3rd to 5th grade**, to becoming a day scholar from **6th to 10th grade**, life kept pulling me away from her.

We rarely had dinner together. We rarely shared time as brother and sister. And when I finally went back to hostel life in **11th grade**, the distance grew again.

I missed so much.

I missed moments that could have become memories.

I missed the small things, the everyday things, the things that stay in the heart forever.

Those lost memories... I can never get them back. And even today, that truth still hurts.

In those three years of my life, I lost countless small seconds - seconds that could have grown into memories, laughter, and stories I could carry forever.

Instead, they slipped through my fingers before I even knew how precious they were.

And somewhere in that quiet loss, a part of me kept wishing I could go back, just to live those little moments I never got the chance to create.

Today, I feel the opposite of what I once did. Back then, when I was in the hostel, all I longed for was my family. Now, standing years away from those corridors and those nights, I find myself longing for the hostel life I once wished would end.

It is strange how our hearts work - we always miss something that belongs to another time, another place. Yet when we are actually living in that moment, we rarely understand its value.

Why is it that we only realise the worth of a place when we no longer belong to it?

Don't know why...

The lessons I carry from those three years have become my compass for life.

They taught me what true bonds feel like,

what real friendship means,

and how to look fear in the eye and understand it instead of running away.

I cannot imagine who I would be without those three years of courage and discovery.

From 2008 to 2010, those days shaped me in ways I am still learning to understand - and they continue to guide me even now.

That school life was not just a phase - it was the foundation on which I was built.

It shaped me quietly, day after day, teaching me strength, patience, and the meaning of standing on my own.

Everything I am today has a piece of those years in it.

When I look back, I realise it was those moments, those struggles, and those small joys that carved me into who I have become.

Even today, there is a small ache in my heart - a question that never really leaves me: why couldn't I hold on to the friendships I made in school?

Maybe it's just who I am. I've never been someone who makes friends easily, and at 24, I can finally admit that about myself.

But somewhere inside me, a part of that 7-year-old boy still exists... the boy who wanted to belong, who tried to understand the world, who wondered why friendships slipped away. And thinking of him still makes me smile, and hurt, at the same time.

I have always wished to stay connected,

to hold on to **my friendships**,

to carry **people** with me as I grew.

But somewhere, inside my own world of thoughts, I kept drifting away. Not intentionally… but quietly, slowly. And before I realised it, I had left people behind - friends who mattered, moments that could have lived longer.

It is something I still think about, something I still feel.

Epilogue

Where Childhood Ends… and Life Begins

The Green Board had long been wiped clean.

The chalk dust had settled.

The applause had faded into the walls.

But the echoes stayed.

Aarav stepped out of Sarvani Vidya Nikethan not as the frightened boy who once clung to Vihan's hand, but as a child carved by laughter, rivalry, friendship, fear, rebellion, courage, and the fragile first sparks of connection. The hostel gates closed behind him, yet the world inside them refused to let him go.

To the others, it might have looked like an ending.

To Aarav, it felt like a quiet beginning he didn't fully understand yet.

Because childhood never ends in one moment.

It ends in pieces -

in a farewell whispered to a rival,

in a smile exchanged with a friend who never said out loud how much she cared, in promises made under dim corridor lights,

in fears broken on the 60th morning,

in laughter shared in bathroom battles,

in stories unfinished… like the movie that was switched off too early.

Aarav carried all of it with him:

Zia's calm presence that steadied his storms.

Selena's rivalry that forced him to rise.

Vihan's unwavering brotherhood that held him tight.

Sampath's innocence, Akhil Sai's mischief, Akhil's quiet seriousness -

the trio who transformed ordinary days into legends.

He didn't know what came next.

But he knew something had changed forever.

One day, he would return - not as the 7-year-old who feared Hindi class, nor as the boy who longed for the Green Board, but as someone life had shaped in ways hostel walls could never see.

Would Zia's path cross his again - perhaps in a college corridor where destiny decides to play its own script?

Would Selena's storm ever quiet into something softer than rivalry?

Would the boys who once turned bathrooms into battlefields find their way back to the laughter they left behind?

Life rarely gives answers early.

It gives clues - tiny, delicate, hidden between pages.

*And this book closes not with **certainty**, but with **possibility**.*

Because Aarav's story was never meant to end here.

Childhood was only the first act.

The real story - the one life had been patiently preparing him for - waits just beyond this page.

He doesn't know it yet.

But the next chapter begins the moment this one ends.

And somewhere, in a future yet to unfold,

the boy who once looked back at a blank Green Board

will step into a world where lessons are no longer written in chalk -

but in choices, in courage, in love, in loss,

and in the kind of friendships that survive distance and time.

This is not the end.

This is the pause before the world opens again.

Aarav's journey continues… in Part 2.

Foundations of the Story.

Venugopal Rao Killamsetty & Gita Killamsetty

My parents

Foundations of the Story.

Praneeth Killamsetty (as Vihan in the story)

My Brother

Author Biography

Sravanth Killamsetty is an entrepreneur by profession and an author by passion. With prior experience as a co-author on multiple published works, he now steps forward as a solo author with this deeply personal non-fiction narrative drawn from real life.

An engineer and MBA graduate, Sravanth blends analytical clarity with emotional honesty, creating stories that are both reflective and grounded. His writing is rooted in truth, memory, and lived experience. Hailing from the village of **Garabandha**, Odisha, his upbringing continues to shape his voice and perspective.

Connect with him on Instagram at **@sravanthonline** or via email at **killamsettysravanth.96@gmail.com**.

Acknowledgment to Readers.

Thank you for walking with me through the hostel days - through friendships that shaped us, bonds that felt pure, and rivalries that taught us who we were becoming.

These pages carry memories once lived in laughter, silence, and longing. If any moment here felt familiar, if it stirred a memory of your own, then this story has found its place.

Thank you for being part of this journey.

About the Author

Sravanth Killamsetty, Author

(in & as Aarav)

Instagram: @sravanthonline

Mail: killamsettysravanth.96@gmail.com

Friendships do not all share the same fate - some drift away, some remain constant, and some return when you least expect them.

What if Aarav returned someday, walking through the same corridors not as a boy, but as someone changed - yet carrying the same spark in his eyes?

What if Zia's calm presence and gentle smile were to cross his path again, not in a classroom, but in the whirlwind of college life - two old friends meeting as if destiny had saved a chapter just for them?

What if the laughter of Sampath, Akhil Sai, Akhil, and all the others came alive again, as they reunited to write more memories, louder and brighter than before?

These questions linger like shadows of the past, waiting to become light in the future. Because life rarely ends with a full stop. It ends with a comma - leaving space for the story to breathe, to return, to surprise.

Aarav's journey is not over.

Friendships, rivalries, pranks, heartbreaks - these were only the first act of a much larger play.

The truth is - The story has not ended.

It has only taken a break.

And somewhere, beyond the last page of this book, the next chapter is already waiting.

Part Two explores the life that followed the hostel years and everything that changed after 2010.